Sacred Time Management

HeatherAsh Amara

Other books by HeatherAsh Amara and Raven Smith

The Four Elements of Change
The Toltec Tarot
Spiritual Integrity
Awake!
Toltec Recapitulation

Toltec Center of Creative Intent
www.tolteccenter.org
512-233-8480

First edition

Sacred Time Management

Daily Prayer

May I clear my mind of all thoughts
And focus my intent on stillness.

May I clear my field of busyness
And connect to my deepest faith.

May I open my emotional body
And allow healing flow.

May I honor this physical form
As a sacred temple.

May I walk my highest purpose
With gratitude
For this precious time.

Table of Contents

Chapter 1 - What is Your True Work?

Satima, or SAcred TIme MAnagement, is the art of cultivating more connection to spirit in each moment. When we live our life as art we make room for creativity, flow, connection, synchronicity, and magic. We learn to slow down internally and make choices not from our fear, but from our stillness.

In the Western world we are trained to use our brains and our will to power through whatever needs to be done. As we become a more technological society and the speed of our communication increases, so does our own frantic pace to keep up. So many of us spend our time overwhelmed, feeling behind, frustrated, and never getting to the projects that lie in our heart. We cram meals and spirit in between work and getting the kids to school on time and paying bills. Our jobs become filled with drama or exhaustion or rote behavior. Our spirit begins to diminish from lack of nourishment.

A dear friend and mentor shared a story that embodies the poignancy of our need for change in our relationship to work. She is a professional, sought after teacher with students around the world. She travels constantly doing what she loves. And she confessed to me her own burn out.

"I went into teaching to support my spiritual path, but now I notice that my life is, 'did the Germans get the flyer?' 'What workshop should we do in the Spring?'" She laughed and said "All I wanted to do was meditate, and now I have a farm!" She told me this story:

A monk and his disciple spend their days in silent meditation. One day the master leaves, telling his disciple he will be back sometime in the future. A couple of days go by and the disciple realized he is hungry. He decides to go out and buy a cow so he can have milk. He goes back to meditating. Then he realizes he has to feed the cow. So he buys some seeds and plants hay for the cow. The crop grows, and he needs help harvesting it. So he gets married. He has children. The family needs a home so he builds a house and gets more cows. They also plant a garden, and get some chickens. Years later the master arrives to find a whole farm where there once was only two men sitting in meditation...

We go into our work sometimes because we must, and sometimes because it is our joy. Yet how often do we end up swamped, not fulfilled, or burned out? Overwhelm and burnout is epidemic in all types of work, from corporations to massage therapists, retail stores to spiritual teachers.

I deeply understand this dilemma, as I am a recovering overwhelmer. I founded and ran a spiritual center in Berkeley, California that began as a group of five beings starting a spiritual nonprofit. Soon it had blossomed into numerous apprenticeship programs, a teaching program, ten circles across the country, a staff, payroll, board meetings, and outreach programs. It was a joy to make my dream come true, and I soon learned that my foundation was out of alignment with my vision.

Over time what started as a spiritual blessing drained my energy, dissolved my enthusiasm, and left our entire staff exhausted and frustrated. This was not due to the Center or the staff or the amount of work, but to my own unconscious structures and how they had woven through our organization.

When we closed the Toltec Center in Berkeley I went on a quest to discover how to shift my relationship with work. What I learned over the last year of the Center's existence and in the years since are the core of the Satima principles.

No matter how exciting and service oriented your work may be, if you do not clear out old habits they will compromise all that you do. This principle also applies to all of your relationships.

If you do not enjoy your work, clearing out your old belief systems will bring you a sense of ease and fulfillment, no matter what you are doing.

If you are planning to leave your boring corporate job to pursue your dreams you will re-create similar dynamics and issues if you do not also focus on cleaning up your own old agreements.

Satima is not about better tools to make you a faster, more efficient business machine. It is a complete rewiring of your system, a foundational shift. Satima cuts through old programming, fear, and survival strategies and invites you to start making choices from your essence rather than your head. It invites you to use the workplace (and the rest of your life!) to explore and unweave tangled energetics in your being. It asks you to take responsibility for your creation. It asks you to be more intimate with yourself, to live from your depth instead of your crust.

When we live from our crust we follow unconscious habits and patterns, or simply model ourselves after what everyone else is doing. In Sacred Time

Management we start with bringing awareness to these behaviors as a means to more conscious choice and depth. The behaviors include:

- Needing other people's approval
- Believing you have to do everything perfectly
- Taking responsibility for other people's actions and feelings
- Not being clear with your agreements between yourself and others
- Not attending to financial realities
- Procrastinating and avoidance
- Trying to control situations and people
- Keeping busy and productive to prove you are a good person
- Using punishment /guilt/shame to keep yourself or others in line
- Needing to be right
- Distracting yourself from the true work

We start with the foundational question of Satima: What is your true work?

Did you really incarnate to spend much of your time playing out the agreements in the list above? To be stressed out in your wonderful life? To feel impotent that you are not living your fullest potential?

We do a funny mind twist around this question of "What is your true work?" I've heard myself think it, and it comes up in my students all the time. "Well, when I finish this project/job/phone call/career then I'll do what I really want/figure out what I want to do with my life/do my spiritual practice. " Or "it will get better," even though it has changed little over the years…

We have bought into the dream that if we only work hard for 40 years or so, then we will have a nice break and we can relax. We have bought into the belief that if we only stay productive, everything will work out (we will get to go to heaven.) We have bought the thought that we have to be perfect in order to be loved, and this causes us STRESS!

Your head may say, "Oh I don't believe those things." But look deeper into your actions. If you are living your true work, are you doing so with ease and joy? If you are searching for your true work, how are you using your situation against yourself?

What would it be like to feel centered, deeply present, and intimate with yourself in all aspects of your life? This is true Sacred Time Management. Each moment is precious, a gift. Sacred Time Management teaches us to unweave the gunk that creates heaviness and stress in our days, so that the purity of each moment may shine through.

Ask yourself what would Sacred Time Management feel like in your day? What would need to change? This chapter is like a magic spell, a new seed… let it infuse your life with more awareness and clarity around your true work.

Satima is about the willingness to go deeper, to expose our old agreements, and to clear them that we may live from our Center, no matter what we are doing.

The funny thing is that once we do the work to untangle we discover more space, more joy, and more productivity! It is a win/win situation!

But oooh your belief systems are not going to let you go easily. Satima is not a one-time quick fix, but a lifetime commitment to yourself. Satima will teach you how to:

- Get clear on your goals and purpose
- Honor your time as sacred
- Honor yourself as sacred
- Enjoy your work, no matter what it is
- Move beyond busyness, stress, overwhelm to joyous creation
- Act from your internal stillness
- Connect with infinite possibility and her sister, synchronicity
- Make choices that support you in the long term
- Be fulfilled, in this moment
- Have a sense of completion and success always!

Here is your true work: to become as clear a channel as possible so you can align with your spirit, and truly co-create with the God/Goddess/Divine. Let's get started!

HOW TO USE THIS BOOK AND
THE SATIMA PRAYER

This book is divided into two sections. The first half focuses on the teachings of the Satima prayer, which I originally wrote as a way to help me stay grounded with the principles of sacred time management.

> *May I clear my mind of all thoughts*
> *And focus my intent on stillness*
>
> *May I clear my field of busyness,*
> *And connect to my deepest faith*
>
> *May I open my emotional body*
> *And allow healing flow*
>
> *May I honor this physical form*
> *As a sacred temple*
>
> *May I walk my highest purpose*
> *With gratitude*
> *For this precious time.*

Each of the first five chapters of Sacred Time Management focus on one stanza of the prayer, and guide you in how to take its wisdom deeper into your life. The following six chapters explore practical ways to transform your relationship to work, and especially your relationship to yourself.

The Satima prayer will benefit you the most powerfully when you say it out loud in the mornings before you start work. Repeating the prayer each day will allow it to bypass your conscious mind and seed in your subconscious, where it can begin to unwind the structures of stress and overwhelm.

When you speak each line feel the energy and intent

behind the words, and consciously create the state of each word in your body.

I've found that after doing the Satima prayer for two years it has started to do me! When I get stressed or busy the words of the prayer now happily show up uninvited, a sweet angel at the door reminding me to clear my mind or honor my physical form.

Invite the angel of peace into your heart by integrating the Satima prayer and teachings into all aspects of your life, from work to family, mind to body, and everything in-between. And enjoy the process!

Chapter 2 - Clear Mind

May I clear my mind of all thoughts
And focus my intent on stillness

Our internal dialogue is comprised of the many voices in our head. They distract, judge, compare, and appear to support us in solving problems. These voices take us out of the present, causing us to cycle old thoughts and memories about the past and worries or strategies around the future. Instead of being able to attend to what is actually in front of us, our internal dialogue snags our attention in a mess of stories and dramas.

Learning to consciously direct our mind and stop our internal dialogue will allow us to soften into each moment and open to all possibilities.

Deepak Chopra writes: "In stillness, inner energies spontaneously wake up and bring about the appropriate transformation for every situation." When we bring our attention to stillness we tap into our knowing, which is based in love and infinite choice, rather than our thinking, which is often based in fear and scarcity. Within stillness rests our innate connection to Spirit and our sacred creativity.

Stopping our internal dialogue can take many different forms. Some great allies are: 1) giving our mind something specific to focus on (an affirmation or a chant), 2) using proper punctuation, and 3) taking more mental breaks. We will look at each of these in more detail now, and we will also explore a fourth method, which is stopping the thoughts before they arise. Use them all!

FILL THE SPACE

When you give your mind a chant or an affirmation, you fill the brain space your random thoughts would normally occupy. If you can bring your attention fully to the chant or affirmation you will begin to feel the silence between each word. You must be firm in coming back to your chosen words over and over again, and letting the stillness between the words permeate you. I like to start my mornings off with chanting, and then take one chant into my day. An affirmation can be one word or a sentence: anything from "peace, peace, peace" to "May I open to all possibilities."

PUNCTUATE!

Proper punctuation is another invaluable tool for stopping the internal dialogue. We tend to string together huge run-on sentences in our heads, weaving together our fears of the past or future with present events or triggers. We will do crazy things like talk to ourselves about how we should not be having any voices in our head and then tell ourselves stories about what that means! For example have you ever noticed yourself thinking in a circular, tangled fashion such as this:

"The voices in my head are so loud, I am comparing myself to people around me all the time, I can't get still, I just keep thinking and thinking—Will I ever get this right? What if I can't get quiet? I'll never be able to go any farther on my spiritual path until I still my mind, but it is impossible! My mind is totally out of control. Darn, I forgot to get toilet paper at the store, I always forget something. I am a terrible warrior (priestess, healer, teacher, human being….) If only I could be still inside. I hate my mind! I'm never going to have any peace…." Blah blah blah!

No wonder we are constantly filling our time with talking to others or watching TV or fantasizing! Our mind comments on everything, even about itself! By learning to use a period and stop the next thought, we create space. For the example above, image hearing "The voices in my head are so loud!" And then saying "PERIOD!" Stop yourself right there and take a breath. Do not let any more thoughts squeeze in. "The voices in my head are so loud, PERIOD." Do not allow your mind to comment on this statement or justify it or whine or judge. Do this about a couple hundred times a day or so, and you will notice many more gaps in your thoughts. Keep strong punctuation!

TAKE BREAKS

Get habituated to taking breaks during the day to sink into silence; when going to the bathroom, while eating, in between meetings or clients. Instead of running from thing to thing, thinking all the time, breathe into your feet. Notice the colors around you. Slow down. Walk more slowly between places. Reconnect with silence consciously.

BEFORE THOUGHT

Practice, practice, practice. Silencing the mind takes awareness and the commitment to keep coming back to stillness over and over again. A daily meditation practice can greatly increase your capacity to find silence during your day. I recommend you set an alarm for your practice (start with five to ten minutes and build up to a half an hour), and begin by simply letting your thoughts float by without attaching to them. You do not need to stop them; simply let them pass without judgment.

A more advanced technique is to stop the thoughts before they arise. I sit and imagine the foundation of where my thoughts arise from: to me it looks like a grey-brown field. I can actually feel it in my head. From this field thoughts bubble up. By using my intent I can stop them from arising at all. At first they pop out of the field spontaneously, but over time I have learned to feel and witness when a thought is about to arise and gently send it back down into the silence. Over time you can build your capacity to keep the thoughts from being born.

SATIMA PRACTICE

- Say the Satima prayer out loud each day, pausing at the first stanza, "*May I clear my mind of all thoughts and focus my intent on stillness.*" Settle into the stillness both within and around you. No matter how loud your mind is or what is happening outside, drop deeper into the stillness that lies beneath the noise.

- At work explore acting from your intuition rather than from your mind. Make a commitment to not worry about decisions, but to slow down and listen to what the next best action is.

Chapter 3 – Faith

May I clear my field of busyness
and connect to my deepest faith

Our thoughts strongly affect our physical and energetic bodies, which in turn affect our thoughts. Busy, crisis-oriented thinking causes our body to release adrenaline to prepare us to respond with fight or flight. Any thoughts of "There is not enough time. I cannot handle this. It is too much. How can I manage?" send us into a kind of emergency mode, so even small things seem overwhelming.

We modern day humans often feel like we have to keep busy as a way to prove our worth, or to distract us from our deeper emotions and fears. As everything continues to speed up with the use of email and cell phones, we often feel like we are constantly behind.

Energetically our being gets buzzy and weakened as our bodies soak in the hormones of stress. We become less present, less creative, and more apt to struggle without even realizing we are doing so!

SOOTHING OUR ENERGY

When we make a commitment to clear our field of busyness, we do so by first quieting the mind. With our focus on stillness, we can now delve into smoothing out our energetic being. It has been ruffled! Quieting the mind allows us to perceive the subtleties of the energetic body.

The practice of clearing the energetic field begins with awareness. Take a few moments each day before you do the Satima prayer to sit quietly and open your sensory awareness to your energy body. How does it feel? Calm? Prickly? Buzzy? Tattered? Whole? Armored? Use all of your senses to explore the egg of energy around your body that is the invisible manifestation of you.

By listening and paying attention to your energy body over time you will learn when it is agitated, when it is rooted, or when it needs your attention. Notice how your mind and emotions affect your energy being, and vise versa. What happens to your energy body when your immune system is weak, or when you have a big emotional release? What do you perceive on the energetic level when you have a great, fulfilling day, or take something personally?

As you speak the second stanza of the Satima prayer, "May I clear my field of busyness," breathe out any agitation in your energy being. Notice where you have any fear, anxiety, or are leaning into the future or past. Come present, into this moment, and smooth any jagged edges. Call up an image or action that works for you; for example, tracing your energy body with your hands to smooth it down, or visualizing filling in any holes or tears with light. Take strong, deep, full breaths and let them go completely. Ground yourself into the earth. What do you need to do to bring more calm and wholeness to your energetic form? Experiment!

FIND YOUR CORE FAITH

Once you feel a shift in your energetic field, move deeper into your own core. No matter how tiny the shift is, acknowledge it, and continue to build on this transformation from jittery or guarded to peaceful and open! What do you have faith in? Keep moving beyond any thoughts or stories to the feeling sense of faith. You may have words associated with faith, such as "May this situation work out to benefit everyone," or "My faith is in the Goddess," or "I trust everything is unfolding perfectly." Or there may be no words. In either case, keep moving towards the feeling sense of faith in your body. Breathe this in. Feed it.

By doing this practice as part of your Satima prayers each day, you will begin to nourish calm faith rather than feeding worry or "I can't." In this way your love will begin to guide you, rather than your fear. Your decisions will begin to come from a deeper place within you, more in alignment with your soul. In this way you energetically co-create with the universe with ease and sweetness. Enjoy!

SATIMA PRACTICE

- Say the Satima prayer out loud each day, pausing at the second stanza, "*May I clear my field of busyness and connect to my deepest faith.*" Notice how your energy feels; is it buzzy, calm, excited, dull? Consciously breathe out any busy, buzzy energy. Then name what you want to put your faith into. You can put your faith into God, into life, into the power of unconditional love, or into your capacity to create change. Really let yourself feel your faith.

- Begin to track where you put your energy each week. What are you doing with your time? Include everything you do, from getting ready in the morning to preparing for work, from eating to business meetings. You can use your current day planner/calendar to jot down what you do each day, or create a spreadsheet in increments of 15 minutes so you can explore your relationship to time throughout the day.

- Practice simply witnessing your actions, rather than judging them or telling yourself stories.

Chapter 4 - Fluidity

May I open my emotional body
and allow healing flow

As one of the most important and powerful forces of life, water can both nourish and wreak havoc in nature. From gentle mist to violent flooding, from a good cleansing rain to hurricanes, from our mother's womb to the salty seas, this vital element embodies all aspects of life.

Our emotional body is as diverse and powerful as water. From sweet tears of joy to furious rage, emotions span the oceanic breadth and depth of human experience. As pure energy, they are best in flow.

Sacred Time Management honors that we are fluid, changing beings, not robots. Our focus is not on how to squeeze more work out of our being at whatever cost to our emotional and physical being, but to learn to open to all the unexpected events that touch on our emotions: the computer breakdowns, the death of someone close to us, a fixed deadline, with natural grace.

This chapter we focus on two aspects of flow; exploring the tasks and to do's as flowing energy that requires a structure to contain and direct its movement, and learning to allow emotions to move through us effortlessly.

YES, IT IS ENDLESS!

Your to do list is not going to be completed someday so you can rest. The mentality of, "If I just work really hard now I can retire in 10 years and enjoy my life," is destructive to the sacredness of the now. Any fixation you have on getting it all done so you can let go only gives you permission to abuse your body, mind, and spirit in the present for some future goal. As the saying goes, the end does not justify the means. Life is for living in this moment. The things to "accomplish," both little and small, are part of the flow of life, not something to complete before living.

When you deeply understand on a cellular level that all types of work - from your job, to your spiritual path, to the maintenance of your physical body - are like a river rather than a weight, you can open and respect the flow. Imagine joyfully surfing the waterways of information and actions with a twinkle in your eye, rather than feeling constantly on the verge of drowning!

Awareness is the key. Pay attention to how you relate to the liquid of stuff that needs your attention in one way or the other. Do you spend all of your time on the next emergency: frantically trying to bail out your life with a paper cup while the chaos overflows over everything and wreaks havoc? Do you try and control things with force and exhaust yourself without ever getting anything done because all of your energy is tied up in struggle and fight? Do you ignore things until they stagnate and creates stinky piles?

NEW STRUCTURES

Once you have a metaphor for how you are handling the flow, consciously invite in images and vision of how to best direct it. What structure is needed? Create a temporary dam by taking some space to look at the bigger picture. Where could you create structures that would allow the flow to happen with a minimum of energy on your part? If you do specific actions over and over what would help to standardize it? If there is an area of your world that always feels flooded or stagnant what tools can you bring to bear at the source of the problem?

The intent is to shift you from surviving to a sense of masterful surfing. This takes being willing to look at source solutions rather than using band-aids and duct tape. Keep encouraging your brain to look for creative, fun solutions. Your brain plugged into spirit is an amazing ally! Ask yourself, "What would make this flow in the long term? Put your energy towards sustainability and overall vision of sweet fluidity, then take action to put the structure into place! Gather tools and resources from others to inspire you to find what best works for YOU! Be willing to change and explore with the focus on structures that create more spaciousness and ease.

HONORING EMOTIONS

Now, about your inner river of emotions. Many beliefs and experiences cause us to lock down our emotional capacities; being told we should not cry or be angry, fear that if we express the emotion we will hurt others, a belief that spiritual people do not have erratic emotions. Emotions are sometimes treated as a child that no one wants to claim. Like all neglected children our distaste or avoidance causes confusion, rebellion, and pain.

Befriending our emotional body takes patience and a

willingness to be messy. It is the willingness to sit quietly in the corner with the cobwebs and dirt and invite the abandoned child of your emotions to speak. It is the willingness to open your throat and unlock your jaw and make noise, even when you do not want to. It is the willingness to be honest with yourself about the areas where you are using a story to stimulate emotions to avoid a deeper truth. It is the willingness to let whatever needs to arise come up to the surface and be released.

So many of our strategies are designed to block or moderate our emotions so they are "acceptable" or non-existent! Lack of emotional flow causes heaviness to build in our body, which dulls our creativity and passion. When we stagnate or distort our emotions this vibration ripples out to affect our mental, energetic, and physical bodies. Old emotions from the past are stored in our tissue, and need to be consciously brought into the light and released.

This does not mean that you must remember every time you stuffed an emotion, or understand every wave of grief or anger. Flow is flow, it does not need the mind to analyze or correct. Emotions, like water, want to move. The mind often wants to create dams to stop this flow out of fear. Working with the emotional body is about slowly dissolving these mental dams and beginning to guide the flow rather than trying to control it.

Willingness is vital to creating the space for emotional healing. By simply stating each day "May I open my emotional body and allow healing flow," you are giving your being permission to release the past. As you say the prayer feel into your body and notice if there is any place you are holding tension or blocks in your body.

Breathe into these areas. Often we lock emotion in our shoulders, chest, stomach, or back. Grief is often held in the chest, anger in the back, fear in the stomach area. Begin to look for the places you tense your body to stop emotions. One good place to focus is on keeping the jaw relaxed. Aaaahhhh.

Be willing to allow whatever emotions to arise. Don't analyze! Experience and keep it moving. You do not have to experience big catharsis, simply breathing more space for flow will move emotional energy. Sometimes we hope that we will just have one emotional experience, and then we will be done. But emotions take their own time and space to be expressed. Be patient. Keep the door open. Move your body and use your voice to free the emotional pathways within you. They are energy, pure and simple.

As you clear old heavy emotional energy out of your being you can begin to use your feeling sense as a wonderful gauge. Your intuition taps your emotional body to express its message. But when your emotional energy is not cleaned from the past, it is like peering through old gunky windows. You cannot see clearly. When information does come to you, it becomes muddled and misinterpreted.

This is one of the fabulous benefits of attending to your emotional body. Not only will you be more adaptable and filled with more energy and strength, you will also be more attuned to the subtleties of your intuition. This is vital in Sacred Time Management. Instead of being busy to avoid emotions, you will learn to quietly tune into your emotions as a guide and teacher. Instead of something to be feared or controlled, your emotions are a vital component of learning to move beyond time and lists, and into action connected with the wisdom of your knowing.

SATIMA PRACTICE

- Say the Satima prayer out loud each day, pausing at the third stanza, "*May I open my emotional body and allow healing flow.*" Scan your internal being and invite any emotion that may be blocked to loosen and be released. Breathe in pleasure and joy, allowing these emotions to permeate the water in your body.

- Spend time this week visualizing everything you have to do as fluid liquid. What kind of container or sacred structure will best help you direct its power?

- Befriend your emotional body. Tell yourself you are open to all your emotions, and create safe space to simply be so you can create the space for emotional flow. A great way to move emotions is through dance. Turn on your favorite music and let yourself express. You do not need a specific goal in mind, be curious. Pretend you are a fierce animal. Play with dancing a particular emotion with all of your love. Imagine you can shake out anything that no longer serves you. Explore! Give yourself permission. This is not the permission to dump your emotions on others, but to take complete responsibility for maintaining your inner flow and peace.

Chapter 5 - Grounded Presence

May I honor this physical form
as a sacred temple

With Sacred Time Management gone are the days when you can pretend you are simply a machine of productivity and ignore the stress, pain, and needs of your body. Satima integrates all parts of you, including your physical being. You are not just a mind checking off the next thing on your list or a tool for getting things done physically. Your body has wisdom and valuable information threaded through every cell and organ. The physical body is the foundation of sacred time, not the limiting factor we often treat it as.

You can use your physical form as the anchor for showing up in the now: in this place and this time. You create stress by not being present with the body and rushing towards the future. Take a moment to feel how your body reacts when you say to yourself over and over again, "How will I ever get this all done?" or when you get confused or overwhelmed around work. Probably your muscles tense, your heart rate increases, and you stop breathing. This sends the internal message, "Something is wrong!" which causes the body to continue to gear up for flight or fight. Over time you train the body that missing a phone call or not getting something done in time is almost on the same level as a major physical threat. This is not happy-making to the body and leads to chronic ailments and exhaustion.

It can be very challenging to break this pattern, since

most of the people around you hold stress in their body around work. Imagine if everyone around you responded to work "emergencies" with faith, calm, and a relaxed body. Yum! Since this is not usually the case, treating your body as a sacred temple means rewiring yourself to relax physically through anything that arises, including tight deadlines, angry customers, or piles of work. All this in spite of what anyone else around you is might be doing. Here are a few ways to re-align with your physical body to bring healing and unlock the wisdom within.

EARNING YOUR BODY'S TRUST

When you do not properly care for your body, it simply stops trusting you. Symptoms include: You breathe shallowly. You keep your shoulders hunched and muscles tight when you work. You forget to take breaks to unwind or eat. You do not sleep enough. You do not exercise. All of these small acts add up and tell your body over and over again: "You do not matter."

My yoga mentor, Ana Forrest, calls all forms of self-abuse "self-mutilation." Self-mutilation ranges from simple unconscious disregard to active self-hatred. It includes the subtle shades of unconscious actions like eating the wrong foods for your body or comparing yourself to another, to the obvious symptoms, such as anorexia or cutting yourself.

Regaining your body's trust is vital to living in a sacred way and being more efficient with your work. Clear out any beliefs you have that say, "In order to get things done you must ignore your body." Banish the thoughts that your body is an obstacle! There is nothing more powerful at work than a human whose mind, spirit, AND body are in harmony. To reclaim this harmony, start small. Breathe and consciously relax your body many times during the day. Get enough sleep. Eat foods that nourish you. Get enough exercise for your body.

What does your body need? Take on one area at a time. If it needs eight hours of sleep, make this a priority. If you need to shift your diet put your attention there. Again, pick one area to focus on at a time. If there is an area that you do not have control over (perhaps you have a baby so sleep is erratic) be creative in your solutions, or put your attention on really nourishing yourself in other areas.

The focus is on nourishing and honoring your body through stressful situations, so that what you perceive as stressful, shifts. Keep asking for support and guidance and it will come. A few years ago I went on retreat by spending a week alone in our RV, parked outside of the house. I took the time to slow down, to write, and to do some inner work. The third day in I overheard my husband Raven talking on the phone about something that needed to be done and my mind freaked out. I was able to witness my mind creating an emergency and my body responding with an overwhelming need to take an action now!! I was the only one who could do the task! I was going to have to come out of my retreat to handle the problem, there was no way around it.

The level of alarm in my body was hugely out of proportion, but very real. By sitting with my experience and staying with the discomfort I was able to laugh at what I was considering an emergency, and put things into much needed perspective. This allowed my body to relax and recalibrate what was actually true vs what my mind said was true. And, indeed, the world was not going to end if I did not take action immediately. Imagine that.

GROUNDED PRESENCE

Practice showing up in the now. Use your senses to ground yourself here. What are the smells around you? How does your body feel? Are you breathing? How does the air feel against your skin? Experience this moment and all of its intricacies. Do not avoid the knot in your shoulder or the ache in your knee. Breathe into your full being and give equal awareness to the places that feel good and the places where there is pain or tension. Straighten your spine, let your shoulders slide down your back, and open your heart to the temple of your body. Be with what the actual experience of your body is, not with how you wish it were. Breathe and open.

From this place of acceptance, connect yourself to the earth beneath you. You can use the image of yourself as a tree and your roots going down into the earth, or of plugging yourself in to a larger source of energy. Grounding your body connects you to the wisdom of nature that we humans tend to disconnect from. Let yourself rest into the feeling that you are being held by the strength of the earth. Tap into the firmness of rock, the flexibility of the trees, the patience of the flower bud unfolding.

DOING THE NEXT THING

Raven started a great game with me that we now play

all the time when we get overwhelmed with our lists. When one of us says "I have too much to do," or "I do not know what to do next," the reply is always a big hug and the words "You only have one thing to do: the next thing on your list."

You can only every really be doing one thing fully at a time. Yes, I know you believe you should be able to do ten things simultaneously. Yes, I know you wish you could do all the steps of a project at the blink of an eye so all you had to do was the final action and you would be done. You probably create way more work for yourself by thinking about the many steps rather than just doing them one at a time!

Do your best, one action item at a time. Do not force yourself to act. Using force to get things done is self-abuse. Force is when you cut from your body and use judgment and aggression to make things happen. Support is when you stay connected to your body and invite yourself to stretch beyond what you thought you could do. When you use force you are taking yourself by gunpoint; when you use support you are taking yourself by the hand with a smile. Force is a short-term solution; support is a long-term relationship of internal respect.

It might look like forcing yourself to act is the only way to stop procrastinating or get through the hard projects, but force always leads to internal rebellion. Either you get sick or lose desire to take any actions at all. Look at your overall relationship to work and begin the transformation from force to support by breaking things apart and making a game of anything that has been a struggle in the past. The game for today is... Go sit under the tree outside and make an outline of the proposal. Or, file this one-inch stack of papers without whining.

Get the energy moving forward in a lighthearted way. I often take big filing projects or taxes with me in a box to a cafe, and the tedious task then becomes a field trip. Fun!

When your body is cared for and supported rather than forced to perform, windows of opportunity will open. A space will appear in your schedule to finish the report. You will be inspired to stay up late one night and put energy into a long-term goal. You will know what the next action is in your bones, and the universe will work with you to make the space happen.

SATIMA PRACTICE

- Say the Satima prayer out loud each day, pausing at the fourth stanza, "*May I honor this physical form as a sacred temple.*" Notice where your are holding tension in your body. Breathe into those areas and release. Focus especially on your belly and your shoulders. Feel your physical body as a sacred temple, one that you are the appointed caretaker.

- In all of your in between times (driving, waiting in line at the grocery store, on the way to the bathroom) tap into pleasure, breathing it through your body. You can link pleasure to this moment by opening your sense and perceiving any tiny thing that brings you pleasure; the wind on your skin, the color of the car next to you. Or recall a time you felt pleasure and bring it into this moment so you are feeling it rather than thinking about it. Practice!

Chapter 6 – Gratitude

May I walk my highest purpose with gratitude
for this precious time

Walking your highest purpose is the foundation of Sacred Time Management. Having a purpose (a specific goal) gives you direction and focus; connecting to your highest purpose aligns you with the Divine and feeds your soul. A goal without connection to a higher purpose can easily lead to stress and worry, as your mind and ego get fixated on obtaining the goal to prove your worth. A goal held within the container of a higher purpose is grounded in joy and faith. Each of your actions becomes infused with the knowing that you are co-creating with the Divine.

If you are not yet sure what your highest purpose is, don't think about it! Your mind will most likely just confuse the issue. Your highest purpose is more of a feeling sense, a knowing, or a phrase that resonates in your bones. Start by picking a word that is your current focus. Close your eyes and go into that word and the feeling behind it, letting the energy of the feeling vibrate and increase through your body. Breathe it into every cell. Listen carefully to your inner self, without thinking.

Once the feeling state is stable in your body, ask yourself: "If I was living from this feeling state all of the time, what would I want to do in the world? What gift would I want to share?" If you drop out of the state and start thinking then stop, settle yourself back into the state, and listen.

You may need to do this exercise over and over again

before you start to get a glimpse of your purpose; for others it will be clear immediately. There is no rush to figure out your highest purpose; let it arise from the center of your being. Keep creating spaciousness within yourself so there is room for your purpose to be heard, trust the process. Let it unfold from the inside out. Keep praying with your heart wide open, "May I walk my highest purpose."

Whether your mind knows what your highest purpose is, your center has never stopped holding your purpose. Whether you have known your highest purpose since you were a toddler, or you are still waiting for the light bulb to come on, keep bringing your awareness to being grateful for what you have. Embodying gratitude changes not only your perception of the world around you, but also your vibration. As you learn to walk more consciously in gratitude for everything that arises in your life, from the challenging to the sublime, you will magnetize the people and situations most in alignment with your highest purpose. This is faith in action.

The last line of the Satima prayer, *with gratitude for this precious time*, invites us to remember that our relationship with our mind, energy, emotions, and body will end one day. We have a finite amount of time to befriend and align all aspects of our being and to blossom into our fullest potential. This second, this minute, this moment are blessings we can use fully or let slip away. Stay conscious of the ways you procrastinate or minimize the things that are really important to you, and the old patterns that cause you to be diverted from your highest purpose.

To clean the channel around your highest purpose, take a few days to explore what internal "prayer" you say to yourself when you go unconscious.

An example would be:

May I avoid punishment

May I do a good job so people like me
May I be productive and busy so I do not feel inferior
May I get this project done so I get a raise

You can catch them by watching your actions and thoughts. For example, if you notice that you say, "I am sorry," all the time, take note of the feeling and thoughts associated with "I am sorry" and see what the actual belief is beneath it is.

The belief might be: "I do not deserve to live," or "I will get hurt if I am too big in the world," or "I can't do anything right."

Now image that part of yourself saying a "prayer" based on the belief. What words would it use? Play with this without analyzing it too much!

May others see my fear and leave me alone

May I be small and invisible, so others will not hurt me
May I do everything perfectly in order to avoid rejection.

By bringing this unconscious mantra into the light you will take away some of its energy and power over you. You can now create a new stanza of the Satima prayer that is tailored specifically for you by rewriting your old "prayer" into a new, conscious one. Here are the transformations:

From: *May I be small and invisible, so others will not hurt me*
To: **May I hold my own power and light, knowing that I am held by the divine**

From: *May I do everything perfectly*
To: **May I do my best in each moment**

From: *May others see my fear and leave me alone*
To: **May I connect with myself and others through my heart**

Ah, much better! As you run into situations that trigger you into the old patterns repeat your new prayer to yourself, over and over again, as you embody the words. As you continue to integrate the five stanzas of the Satima prayer and your self-tailored sixth stanza you will gently re-wire your entire system.

KEEP INTEGRATING!

Continue to say and feel the prayers on a daily basis, and then begin to bring the prayers into your actions. As you exercise, wash the dishes, or drive the kids to school practice saying one stanza. Say it to yourself or out loud, depending on the circumstances, and then shift your state. Can you clear your mind of all thoughts and focus on stillness while you go for a walk? As you move, drop beneath your thoughts and reach out to feel the silence in all things.

As you check your emails can you clear your field of busyness and connect to you deepest faith? If you have a pattern of getting overwhelmed by a particular task this is a good stanza to work with. Set a timer to go off every fifteen minutes or so, take a breathe, say the stanza out loud and clear your field, re-anchor your faith, and move back into the task. Practice, practice, practice!

In dance class, yoga, or while taking a shower explore opening your emotional body. I've noticed when I pray to open my emotional body and allow healing flow and bring my attention to the area in my body where I am holding tension there is a big release of energy. I hold my tears in my upper chest, so I move grief out of my body around my father's death by saying the stanza and then very consciously breathing into my chest and softening the area under my collar bones. Boom, the tears start flowing!

In this way I can be proactive in my relationship to my emotional body instead of pushing past the feelings until a big release moves through. I keep inviting smaller releases and making space for the emotional flow. While driving I bring my attention to letting pleasure and joy run through my body.

As you eat, clip your fingernails, or work in your garden honor your form as a sacred temple. Notice how you hold your physical form. Love and appreciate your amazing body and all it can do. Do not focus on the places you may still abuse or ignore your body, but string together all the little moments of honor and graciousness. Start small: Eat the first two bites of each meal savoring the nutrition in the food and being fully present. When you brush your hair slow down and look yourself in the mirror and send yourself love. As you put on your shoes send blessings to your feet.

All time is sacred, not just the time you are meditating

or doing your spiritual practice. By linking the Satima prayer to all aspects of your life time will expand and become more luscious.

Gratitude....

Chapter 7 – Overcoming Overwhelm

Your body is naturally designed to overcome being overwhelmed. Each second your body processes thousands of different inputs from your internal and external environment and filters out what is not relevant to your functioning in this moment. Feel into the truth: "My body already knows how to do this." Your being has amazing, untapped capacities that you can direct to supporting you in overcoming overwhelm in all areas of your life.

First, the brain. Your mind probably needs some rewiring around how it views your experience. While part of your brain is helpfully assisting your body in tasks like breathing and regulating our blood pressure, a part of your brain is the busy doing other things. It is creating worry, stress, and the sense of being buried under piles of emails, phone calls, and tasks that all need to be done right now. This is the part of your brain you can retrain to calmly sort and choose rather than frantically acting or being paralyzed. Here are four ways you can overcome overwhelm. Yes!

FROM DROWNING TO FLOATING

When we are overwhelmed we shift from conscious choice to a sense of desperate survival. Instead of seeing possibility, we see our core agreements reflected back to us: "I am not good enough," "I can't do it," "I am alone, there is no one to help me." Overwhelmed people often feel and behave if they are drowning. We spend a lot of energy splashing around and looking for something to save us. Often we end up clutching at whatever is around to give us a sense of safety: food, alcohol, taking care of other people.

Or we have the illusion: if I just keep doggy paddling I will be okay. We become consumed by our work and hold the belief that we can only rest when it is all done (or we will surely drown.) Notice how mental thoughts can create a physical sense of panic, which we believe is okay, or we embrace as the energy we need to get things done. Feel the difference between viewing the vastness of the ocean from the perspective of someone who is drowning in it, versus someone who is sitting in a solid boat with a good paddle. Let's shift and find a boat to rest into! From the helm we can then decide which direction to go.

Emotional, mental, or physical overwhelm occurs when we are flooded with too much information without the capacity to sort. We can be overwhelmed with an emotion, overwhelmed with thoughts, or overwhelmed with material stuff. When we feel overwhelmed we experience panic, helplessness, confusion, frustration, or fear.

Take a moment now to go deeper into your own personal relationship with overwhelm. Close your eyes and imagine a time when you were overwhelmed. How does your body feel? What thoughts are you having? Is the flavor one of fear, confusion, or helplessness? Take the time to map out how overwhelm affects you. Awareness of what exactly the impact of overwhelm is for you is the first step in learning to float.

Once you have honed your awareness around your

relationship to overwhelm, let's bring in a new character. Imagine a being that would thrive on overwhelm and rise to the challenge. You might imagine a seasoned sailor with you in your boat, telling you, "Ah, lass these waves are big, but we have what it takes to face this storm. Have no fear!" Or imagine a steady friend or mentor standing next to you, saying, "You can do this, I have faith in you. A little at a time, step by step." Find an imaginary ally that gives your body a sense of calm. Then keep building this relationship internally. Visualization and imagery are powerful tools for interrupting and shifting old energetic patterns.

SELF-SOOTHING

Are you a expert at stirring yourself up into a frenzy? Or accomplished at shutting down and hiding? Whether your coping mechanism is to rush towards or rush away from that which scares you, being with yourself in the present moment is the key to transformation. One way of staying with yourself is self-soothing. As David Schnarch writes in his book, *Passionate Marriage*:

> "Self-soothing involves turning inward and accessing your own resources to regain your emotional balance and feeling comfortable in your body. Your breathing is unlabored, your heart slows to its normal rate, your shoulders are relaxed and no longer hunched to ward off an unexpected blow. Self-soothing is your ability to comfort yourself, lick your own wounds, and care for yourself without

excessive indulgence or deprivation."

Dr. Schnarch's work is geared towards increasing intimacy in relationships. Whether it is with your relationship with other people or with your workload, self-soothing is vital. What do you need to self-soothe yourself through overwhelm? Self-soothing is not about closing down, pushing through the hard things, and then giving yourself a treat for being good. It is about opening to the challenge, as a warrior, with a soft heart and clear eyes and talking to yourself with love, compassion, and patience.

When your judge/victim is running the show and telling you how awful, impossible, unfair, and scary something is you will experience life as one emergency after another. This is not soothing! Explore your own capacity to soothe yourself until this voice is stronger than your disaster mind.

FLEXIBILITY

Increase your perceptual flexibility! When your focus is too broad, you will only see the big picture of all the things that need to be done, making it is very difficult to take action. When you keep your focus too narrow, you will only see the detail of what you are currently working on, making it easy to lose sight of where you are going.

Overcoming overwhelm includes learning how to see the big and little picture simultaneously. You have a good map of your overall projects and you are aware of the next action steps. If you never look at your projects you will be pulled into just doing what shows up in the moment and never get to your bigger projects or goals. If you never pay attention to the details but dream about what it will be like when that your big projects are done, you will keep dreaming!

Put your finger up about four inches in front of your face and focus on it. Now open your perspective to take in the larger view around you. Bring your attention back to your finger. Play with shifting your gaze from your finger to the distance. Just like while driving, you want to split your attention between your dashboard and the road ahead of you. Take an action, then look up!

Keep the context that your actions are moving you towards your bigger goals. Mix doing easy tasks with taking a chunk out of a larger task and completing it. Keep breaking down your projects into smaller and smaller pieces whenever you feel overwhelmed. Be flexible! Relax into the knowing that all projects get completed over time, step by step. Ground yourself in the present, keep your breath full, and stay flexible in your dance between taking actions and reviewing your projects.

This flexibility will also serve you in choosing what task to do next for each of your projects. Take into account your energy level, focus, and time frame when you go to take the next action on a project. Projects often have many steps, not all of them linear. Notice your own rhythms and work with them. You may find you have lots of energy in the morning and hit a slump after lunch. You may want to set up your day so you do brain-oriented or more challenging tasks in the morning and in the afternoon do things that do not take as much of your attention, like your filing or reviewing last week's notes. Move with your own energy while you explore any places you are resisting or being fixated.

One great assistant in gaining flexibility is to use a timer. Pick an action, set your timer, and stop when it goes off. Take a breath. Do not allow yourself to continue on the task; let it go. That is hard, but it is a great practice. Now set the timer again and do something else. Stop. Switch. This will increase your capacity to focus 100 percent on something and then let it go to check in with the bigger picture, or to move another project forward.

WHAT IS RIGHT?

Stop telling yourself what is wrong or undone, and look at what is right! What have you completed? Which tasks did you do this week? What is working for you? The company Peak Potentials has a wonderful slogan: *Celebrate Your Successes!* One of the major culprits of overwhelm is always looking at what is undone rather than what is complete. Take the time to acknowledge yourself when you complete something. Take that in. You did it!

To bring more of a sense of ease and rightness into the repetitive tasks in your life, like housecleaning or filing, remember that this is maintenance, not a project. Projects have a beginning, middle, and end. Maintenance is ongoing action to keep things running smoothly. Maintenance can be a chore, or an ongoing prayer honoring the physical world. It is easy to understand why we need to wash dishes or our hair regularly, yet harder to enjoy. But you can make the shift.

Separate out which things in your life are projects and which are simply maintenance. You will be doing these things over and over and over (unless you hire someone else to do them, which is always an option to look into!) You can bring a sense of overwhelm to maintaining your lifestyle, or a sense of prayer and gratitude. Try holding the rightness of maintenance not as something you need to do perfectly, but as something you bring your love to. When you shift into the flow of maintenance you incorporate it seamlessly into your life rather than it being something else you have yet to complete.

Chapter 8 – Beyond Busyness

Let's start with two visualizations to begin to open to new possibilities.

What would your world look like if you were not busy? Take a mini-retreat in your mind right now. Strip away all of the things in your world that cause you to feel a sense of busyness: email, your in-box, keeping up with your kids, etc. Shed any beliefs that cause you to stay busy to avoid your feelings or appear a certain way to others: lack of self worth, fear, "I must work to be a good valuable human" sorts of things. Can you let yourself relax into not doing?

Dream into living a full year without any sense of busyness. What would you do with your time? How would you interact with other people? How would you feel about yourself? Close your eyes and go deep into exploring life beyond busyness.

Keeping the feeling state alive in your body, and let go of this fantasy completely. You want to use this visualization as a touchstone, not as something to compare your current experiences against so you feel cheated or frustrated that things are not different in your life. Do your best to not use the ideal of never being busy against yourself. Use the feeling state you tapped into to open you to new ways of being in the world. Now you know what you are moving towards.

Bring this feeling state into the present of your current life situation. Imagine that you have the time and energy to accomplish what you want to. There is no need to push yourself or rush. There is space to have a cup of tea with a friend or work on a creative project you have been dreaming of starting. You take action in an unhurried, spacious way. Even if there are many different activities in your day you are present with each one. You are confident, relaxed, and flow gracefully from thing to thing.

Going beyond busyness in a busy world is about changing your perception and internal state. The bee is a great symbol for us to play with. In its natural state a bee is very productive in a focused, present way. If you take a bee and trap it under a glass, however, it becomes frenetic in its efforts to escape. The busyness most of us feel is more akin to the panic of being trapped under a glass rather than the happiness of pollinating flowers or making honey with our actions. The glass that traps us is our mind.

TRACKING YOURSELF

This week set aside four hours (in one chunk or two smaller chunks) where you focus on where you are creating busyness in your life. What steps do you need to take in order to move beyond busyness? Look at the emotional, physical, and mental aspects of your busyness. Do you need to feel something you are avoiding? Do you need to create a new structure? Do you need to switch to a new belief about yourself or the world?

WATCH YOUR LANGUAGE

One major way that we cultivate busyness is through our self dialogue and in our conversations with others.

Take the word "busy" out of your vocabulary completely for a while. Study your speech for any other words that support feelings of scarcity, for any structures that link productivity with being a good person.

Read through the following sentences and notice if any part of you believes them to be true:

If I am busy I will be able to make money
If I am busy I am a good person
If I am busy I will not have to feel my feelings
If I am busy I can stay ahead of feeling guilty
If I am busy I am obviously getting things done
If I am busy I am important or popular

None of them are accurate! Being busy means you are busy, that is all! Do you REALLY want to spend the rest of your life being busy, or being present? Clear out the old language from your speech and internal dialogue. What new agreements do you want to make with yourself around work, beyond busyness?

FINDING FREEDOM IN ACTION

These sort of repetitive thoughts cause you to bump your nose again the invisible glass of your limiting beliefs. Repeat this new awareness: "Outside things are not making me feel busy, I am making me feel busy." Take 100 percent responsibility that it is not the world outside you, but the invisible glass you placed around yourself that is the agitation. Oh, it looks like the busyness is caused by things outside of your control, and yes, they are outside of your control. But you do have control over how you perceive things, and whether you are creating buzz-yness (I am trapped and I can't get enough done!) or bees-yness (I see the next flower and I am heading to it with purpose and joyous focus!) What do you need to do to remove the glass that causes a trapped, panicky feeling?

How have you gotten comfortable bumping up against a familiar barrier of your own making? Sometimes we feel safer keeping ourselves busy, busy, busy in our little contained universe than feeling how much choice and power and freedom we actually have.

Look up! Visualize the limitations, fear, not-enough-time-not-enough-resources-I-am-not-enough   matrix dropping away. Take a deep breathe. Find your center. Motivate yourself out of gratitude and love for each flower you will pollinate with your energy, for the honey you are creating with each action. You are sending your energy out with everything you do; what flavor do you want to imbue it with? What are you pollinating in others by the state you are holding when you do a task?

BEING PART OF A TEAM

Just like a honey bee, you are part of a team of beings working together towards a common goal. Whether at work or at home you are always part of something greater than your individual self. Busyness probably causes you to disconnect. Reach out and feel the web you are part of in the different areas of your life. Who else is part of the project with you? There is the team of your company, the team of your family, the team of other beings doing the same type of work as you in the world.

And fundamentally we are always on a team with Spirit. You are not alone. Learn to delegate, to ask for help, to let others do their part. Who can you rest into? Focus not on where your team is not stepping up, but where they are and how this helps you do your work.

Spirit does not need you to be busy to prove yourself. Magic happens when we listen beyond busyness and allow our actions to be a prayer arising from confidence, faith in ourselves, and a knowing of being part of a march larger dance.

Chapter 9 - Magic Your Mind

Spiritual author Starhawk defines magic as "the ability to change reality through changing your consciousness." The term "magic" is used to express the manifestation of the unexpected, or something that is beyond the mind's capacity to grasp: "It was just like magic!" Happily, you can retrain your logical brain to experience magic and increase the amount of magic floating around your life.

As a child you were probably intimate with magic. As children we often have invisible "magical" friends, and our curious, open minds see possibility rather than limitations. A child-like sense of wonder enhances magical moments; a rigid, logical focus separates us from magic.

A tiny tour of your brain. The left side is called the scientific, logical brain, the right side is your intuitive and creative brain. The ability to methodically interpret and attend to data is the realm of your left brain; the ability to make intuitive leaps and see holistic connections is the realm of your right brain.

To magic the brain means to bring more emphasis on the right hemisphere. For most of us the left, logical hemisphere of our brain runs the show and sometimes we allow the right to peek through. Sacred Time Management takes our relationship with time and moves it from the left to the right, so that our dance with time moves from linear to circular, from limited to flexible. And then magic happens!

Do a quick, magical rewire of your brain right now.

Take your left hand (which is connected to your brain's right hemisphere) and rest it in front of your belly, palm facing up. Take your right hand (which is connected to your brain's left hemisphere) and place it gently on top of your left, palm facing up. Close your eyes and talk to your brain. "Hey up there! We are making some changes. From now on the logical will rest within the intuitive. Scientific brain, thanks so much for you help. You can now relax and be held within the wisdom of my creative brain. We will call you when we need you. Gratitude!"

Keep shifting your alignment away from the logical "There is only one way to do this," towards the creative "How else can I do this?" You want to learn to balance the best of your brain and open the pathway for the miraculous to occur. One way to do this is to engage both your creativity and your intent in the perfect mixture for your current circumstances.

CREATIVE INTENT

Creative intent is your ability to find innovative ways of moving past obstacles while staying focused on your final goal.

Creativity is one polarity of expression, a sense of playful experimentation that stems from dreaming, intuition, and a wide perceptual horizon. Creative energy is the flow of art, and it moves as a spontaneous response to stimuli.

Intent is another polarity of expression, the movement of focused purpose. It is the determined questing of science, and it moves as a piercing force of transformation. Intent stems from disciplined stalking of the goal and strong action to stay on course.

When we have too much intent running, we get narrow-minded and dogmatic. There is no room for discovery or learning through our mistakes. When we live solely from our creativity, we become ungrounded and scattered. We have a lot of ideas, but not the force to manifest them in a concrete manner. It is only when we balance play and focus, discipline and experimentation, intent and creativity, that we possess the ingredients to fully catalyze our blossoming.

Our intent gives us a direction to move towards, and the ability to follow through. Our creativity gets us outside of the narrowness of our domestication and structure, and brings joy to the process of inner alchemy. When we block or judge either energy we cut ourselves off from our full potential.

For those of you who have plenty of creative juice and sense of magic in the world but have a difficult time taking concrete action steps: bring your focus to magical intent infused with action. For those of you who have plenty of focus but not much creative fire: bring your focus to magical vision infused with a sense of play.

QUICK REWIRES

When you notice places that you are stuck in logical thinking, here are a few ways to unstick:

Stand up and bend your right knee to the left while moving your left arm to the right, then switch: left knee goes to the right while your right arm moves to the left. Make sure you cross both your knee and arm over your center line. (Imagine crawling while standing up: that's it!) The movement of crossing over your center line re-links the two hemispheres of your brain and clears new pathways.

Turn on some music with a strong beat and dance wildly! Let your body go all floppy and shake yourself around, then kick or punch the air with focused intent. Keep alternating between fluid and sharp movements. Shake out the stagnation of logic!

Pick one color to focus on and look for all the different hues and shades of that color around you. You can also focus only on shadows or the negative space of objects. Keep this alternative perception going as you interact with the world around you and you will notice your mind opening.

It is also a great idea to nourish your brain cells by doing things like sudoku or crossword puzzles. These keep your brain fresh by exercising your logical and intuitive mental muscles in a fun way. If you get stuck on a project or run out of creative ideas, take ten minutes to work on a puzzle.

COOKING WITH TIME

Madeleine L'Engle, who is most well-known for her book *A Wrinkle in Time*, took a magical approach to writing. She described her writing process as similar to cooking in many different pots at once. She would let some simmer as she added seasoning to another, while others needed occasional stirring. She worked on multiple projects simultaneously, letting intuition guide her when to engage. I love the image of her walking past the pots of her different books, humming as she stirs one, peeking at the one in the back to see how it is doing. There is no force, simply the joy of creation in a magical way.

An interesting note on L'Engle and her work (from wikipedia.com): *A Wrinkle in Time* was written between 1959 and 1960 and published in 1962 after at least 26 rejections by publishers because it was, in L'Engle's words, "too different." The book went on to win a Newbery Medal, Sequoyah Book Award, and Lewis Carroll Shelf Award, and was runner-up for the Hans Christian Andersen Award. A theme often implied and occasionally explicit in L'Engle's works is that the phenomena that people call religion, science and magic are simply different aspects of a single seamless reality.

Where can you use the image of sacred cooking to enhance the flow of magic in your work?

Chapter 10 – Create Clean

Each time you take an action you can make less work for yourself in the long run or more work for yourself in the long run. Creating clean means that you consciously choose to focus on the long term results, with an eye to minimizing future messes. Creating clean focuses on three areas: your core ideology, organizing containers that will hold information/stuff for easy future reference, and clear and timely decision-making and communication.

SELF-ESTEEM AND YOUR CORE IDEOLOGY

A dynamic art of creating clean is finding the balance between your core ideology and your capacity to meet change. Your core ideology is the anchor, the roots that hold you steady on your path. With a solid base set, you can learn to dynamically play with new structures and ways of doing things in a fluid, experiment-oriented way to find what works for you in this moment. The core value is your guiding light, but how you get there will be influenced by your actual experiences.

When you create clean, your decisions are guided by at least two core ideologies: your individual core value AND the core ideology of your company. There is also a third, hidden core value that holds as much, if not more, weight as your individual and company core values; it is how you value yourself.

Beneath any conscious core ideology is the unconscious value you place on yourself as human being. It will be nearly impossible to create completely clean if at your core you devalue yourself. Keep an eye on your own self-esteem with the intent of increasing your core sense of value and worth in the world. Honor yourself for what you do in the world, and know that it makes a difference, no matter how small it may seem. Stop the negative self-talk that says you are not doing enough, you are not doing it right, you are too old; whatever! At your core you are complete and whole and a valuable, unique, precious ray of light in the world.

In their book *Built to Last*, Jim Collins and Jerry Porras explore what it takes to build what they call a "visionary company." These are companies that have thrived over the last 100 years and are the leaders in their field: Johnson & Johnson, Nordstrom, Sony. What the authors discovered surprised them, as it was contradictory to traditional business management. Their research has valuable insights into not only for big companies, but also for small businesses and individuals.

They found that "...what made the difference for the visionary companies were two qualities

1. Strong core values and core purpose
2. The ability to be highly flexible in adapting to change; including their cultural and operating procedures and specific goals and strategies."

This balance of rooted purpose and in-the-moment creativity was the winning combination for visionary companies, and I believe for individuals as well. If you keep increasing your own personal core value, choose a specific core ideology that you operate from, and stay flexible as changes arise, you will always move from your center in a dynamic way.

Knowing what you want to be in the world (or what type of business you want to create) arises naturally from an intent to create a solid sense of yourself as an individual. Take action, experiment, and take in the results. When we take the time to explore how we want to engage in the world, and get the data of what truly excites us, we can then build a firm, clean foundation from that inner knowing. Don't be frustrated if you do not know what you want to do in the world; remember that many of the most successful companies had many failures before they found their niche. You will find your place!

The words or even the focus of your core ideology matters less than your alignment with it, or your own integrity in relationship to your core values.

To explore what the flavor of your core ideology is here are a few from visionary companies to play with:

3M:

Innovation "Thou shalt not kill a new product idea"
Absolute integrity
"Our real business is solving problems"

Johnson and Johnson:

The company exists to alleviate suffering and pain
Decentralization = Creativity = Productivity

Sony:

To experience the sheer joy that comes from the advancement, application, and innovation of technology that benefits the general public

To elevate the Japanese culture and national status

Being a pioneer - not following others, but doing the impossible

Here are some personal core ideologies. Use them as inspiration around your core ideology:

To be the change I want to see in the world

To support others in finding their creative connection to the divine

To heal myself and others of fear and separation

When you name and then align your actions to your core ideology you will stop wasting energy comparing yourself to others or feeling confused. Find out what the core ideology of the company you work for is, or create a set for your own business. Let this be the spine that you act from, both at home and at work.

ORGANIZING CONTAINERS

Each time you engage in a project or task keep your vision on how can I make this clean in the long run? You can easily see the ramifications of not initially creating clean when you look at the places that are messy in your life. If you continuously lose your keys, if your filing cabinet is in disarray, if you can never find that piece of paper you need then the issue is that you do not have a proper container to hold the physical manifestation you are working with, you have a container that needs to be refined, or you need to break down getting things clean into smaller, bite-size steps.

Physical objects
Make a specific place you leave keys, wallet, sunglasses, etc. What do you misplace? It needs a container! Get a physical bowl, hook, or area and be consistent. This is a great mindfulness practice.

Filing Systems
Chunk out your filing system and then alphabetize or consciously sort the chunks. For example, I have three filing cabinet drawers I work out of: TEACHING, PIXIE PERSONAL, FINANCES. I picked these categories based out of what I need to access in the different areas of my life.

Teaching contains anything that has to do with classes, workshops, and clients: My client notes, outlines from workshops, resource information for power journeys, etc.

Pixie Personal contains things like frequent flyer mileage info, old writings, warranties, health insurance info.

The Finances drawer has current and past financial documents, including bank statements, receipts (sorted by category for tax purposes) and old tax documents.

The Teaching and Pixie Personal drawer are alphabetized; the Finance drawer is separated by year and with the most current information I need at my fingertips in the front.

I noticed that one area of messiness in my life was around actually getting things into my filing cabinet. I had a good system but it was not working. For a while I just thought it was because I was being lazy and things kept piling up. But as things continued to pile up I decided to stop and figure out what was going on.

As I sat in my office and stared at the pile of things to be filed that was spilling onto the floor, I reviewed my actions. Why I would put things in this pile rather than in a file? I recognized the problem pretty quickly: because the drawers were hard to get to. Both my filing cabinets are two-drawer and sit on the ground. To file I have to crouch down and open the file, which squeezes me into the desk.

So I decided to run an experiment of stacking the filing cabinets on top of each other and arranging the drawers so that the least used one was at the bottom. Then, since I felt stuck whenever I looked at the pile I called a helpful student to come in and help me clear the old stack and make new files. She was not bogged down by the pile, so she helped get the energy moving as I told her where to put things or what to call a new file. Tada! And now I am noticing that I immediately file something, because it is easy to access the cabinet.

Oh, and I highly recommend getting yourself a personal labeler. Great for labeling files, drawers, spices, cords, etc. They are the best. I have two and am very possessive about them both!

Computer Filing
Create a clean system on your computer. Again, my preference is to have a few main divisions, and then divide things up from there.

I have one main folder for Pixie Personal which includes journaling, poems, stuff that is just for me. Then a folder for our business, Spiritual Integrity, which is divided into Advertising, Audio, Finances,

Office, Teaching, Website, and Writing. Advertising has folders per year, since we do very little advertising, so it does not need to be separated.

Office includes Databases, Marketing, and Templates. Teaching has a folder for each class, workshop, or journey we do, with further folders within for each specific date. My writing folder is divided up into Articles (other people's) Blog (mine) Poems (mine) and different book categories: Satima, Spiritual Integrity, Tarot, etc.

If I find it difficult to find something I know it is either because it is misfiled or I need to create more divisions within my files since they are getting too full. At first it can seem like a pain to move through so many folders to get to an item, but I save a ton of time because I know where they are!

Take your time dreaming into the best system for you, and then once it is set up keep it clean! Put things away as you create them or set up new folders for them. Like your physical filing system if things start backing up you will want to see where the messes are and take appropriate actions.

Be flexible and don't be afraid to try new things and shift them if it does not work. Getting things clean is a work in progress, an art based on interaction between you and your stuff, be it material or binary!

Email Sorting
Make sure you have a very good spam blocker. I highly recommend getting a gmail account if you have a high-speed connection, as their technology to keep spam out

of your inbox is truly phenomenal. I went from deleting hundreds of spam emails a week to only one slipping into my inbox in the past three months! Google's fantastic mail search capacity and archive folder system is also a real timesaver, though it takes a bit to get used to.

This combined with using Google calendar is a beautifully streamlined system, especially if you need other people to check your calendar or add events to your calendar. Google calendar can also be set to email you reminders of upcoming events or deadlines. If you use another on-line service research their offerings and play with what may serve you to be cleaner in your communication and calendars.

In his excellent book, *Getting Things Done,* David Allen recommends that you answer any emails that would take less than two minutes immediately, and then put longer-response emails in an "action" folder. I've found the two-minute rule to be great; and I move not-timely items to either a work or friend folder, which I check once a week. Sometimes things stay in there a long time! However, they are not crowding my inbox, which is nice.

I keep more important, need to answer or take an action emails in my inbox and do my best to not let them pile up. If there is an action item I need to take from an email that is non-email related I make sure to write it down on my action list and then archive or delete the message.

I've also found filters to be very helpful in keeping a clean inbox: with many email programs you can have specific emails sent to a particular folder. There are several groups lists I am on that I want to keep track of but are not time sensitive, so they are all filtered to go into their own labeled folders. Then when I have time I read through these emails. This also keeps the different dialogue trains in order since they are all in one area.

Physical Stuff
Reference materials that are bulky like magazines or stacks of paper can be put in cardboard magazine holders or clipped together and put in boxes and labeled clearly. For things you want to read, create a container for them: a box or clear folder that is marked clearly. If you really are not going to read it, throw it away or file it if it has important reference information.

Projects you are actively working on can be placed in a small hanging file folder or box on your desk, so they are right at your fingertips. I also love clear plastic folders which I use to carry reference materials for projects that are in immediate motion. Other reference stuff that is for longer term projects or stuff I have not gotten to yet lives in a folder in a tray near my desk.

DECISION MAKING AND COMMUNICATION
Creating clean also comes into play around making decisions. Teach yourself to not wait until the last minute to make decision. This is a sloppy habit and will always leave you feeling behind. Start exploring how you can take small steps to get ahead of your deadlines and decisions rather than waiting until the last minute. Be compassionate and lovingly firm with yourself.

Once you have made a decision communicate it clearly

to everyone who needs to know about it. Set aside the time to relay it to the important parties. Much chaos is created by holding back on making a decision or not communicating it succinctly. This often leads to individual stress and can have huge ramifications if you are a major decision maker in your company and everyone is waiting on you. If you need more information, get clear about what the needed information is and get to work finding it! If the decision is an internal one use your breath to slow yourself down and get quiet so the answer can arise.

WHEN YOU CREATE MESSES....

How quickly can you go back and clean things up without beating yourself up? Take note of where the mess is happening and as soon as you are able take the time to correct the problem. Here is where you get to practice flexibility! Learn to backtrack and clean up any messy communication. Notice where you made assumptions. When chaos happens in your office, what is the source? Be tenacious, take responsibility, and try, try again!

Chapter 11 - Succinct, Successful Structures

First, this inspirational quote from Larry Winget, who has been called the "Pitbull of Personal Development."

"Stress comes from knowing what is right and doing what is wrong."

In his oh-so-gentle book *Shut Up, Stop Whining, and Get a Life*, Larry challenges us to change our structure by getting real with ourselves:

> "You know exactly the right thing to do about each of the things on your list. Yes, you do. Do not argue with me. Regardless of what you wrote down, you know... The problem is that you are either doing nothing or you are doing the wrong thing. That is what is causing the stress. It is not the things you wrote down that are causing you the stress at all. It is that you know the right thing to do about them and you are not doing it."

That is succinct! So my challenge to you, inspired by Larry's call to direct action, is to look at what causes you stress and take immediate action based on the solution that is already there, inside of you. Write down what you need to do, and how to do it. What do you perceive causes you stress, and what is the solution?

Then start taking action today based on the solutions you wrote on your list.

BALANCING THE SOLID AND THE FLUID

Sacred Time Management balances making solid, stable

structures with total fluidity and creativity. Structure and fluidity are not opposites, but two aspects of life that are interdependent on each other. Without fluidity structures break apart; without structure fluidity dissolves into nothingness.

I found three places to create succinct, successful structures for myself just yesterday. I was printing out labels for a CD series when I recognized, "oh, yeah, I was going to make a CD of all labels and file this master CD in a specific place so I can always refer to the CD when I need to make labels, instead of needing to search for them on my computer." I'm constantly hunting on my or Raven's computer for our various CD labels, and to have them all together in one CD is a very succinct structure. But it is not successful until I finish the thought! I know what to do... now just do it!

The second was similar, around needing to send a 300 dpi photo to a festival I applied for. As I was hunting around for it on my computer two more succinct structures dropped into my lap: I need a press kit on-line with photos and my bio (yes I've thought about this before and did not act on it), and I need another CD of photos for different medias, from web to print. Next step, the actions to take to create this new structures are now written as action steps on my to do list.

The third is a recognition around a structure I already have in place, but needs some modification. We created a binder for the CDs for our SpiritWeavers program, but the entire binder was missing when I went to find it yesterday. I did finally find it in Raven's room, after a bit of worry that it was somehow lost. The new structure is to have a specific place for it to live so I immediately know if it is missing rather than realizing it is missing after I tear apart my office trying to figure out where I might have stashed it. Now I know exactly where it will live from here on out.

Next part of the structure: let others know who might need it. So here I start a new computer document which lists where important documents/projects live in my office. Succinct!

IMPLEMENT THOSE GREAT THOUGHTS!

Remember the golden rule: Succinct structures are only successful when you implement them! Succinct structures stay successful when you modify them as needed rather than letting them become stagnant.

Yes, all three of the above things caused me stress, and yes, with all three of them I knew the "right" thing to do to relieve the stress: make a succinct structure that would serve me in the future to stop the stress.

Some stressful situations are not stuff-related but people-related. I also believe if we write down the details of the stress and ask ourselves honestly, we know what to do to relieve this stress as well, whether it is to communicate, ask questions, find outside support to get more clarity, or do our own inner work.

I highly recommend that one of the succinct, successful structures you create around you is a team or circle of people who support you, either in your profession and/or emotionally. Find people who are successful, clear, and succinct in their insights. Avoid people who are struggling with similar issues, confused, and like drama. Get clear about what type of support you need to help you move beyond stressful situations and create new structures. Then find it! No whining!

Now I am off to create a label CD, a photo CD, and update my to do list. I suggest you do the same... what is your next succinct, successful structure? Create it now!

Chapter 12 - The Royal Review

To review means to look in a new way, to re-view from a different perspective. There is great importance in re-viewing the components of your life on a regular basis, but the main ingredient is to do your review from a calm, centered, open place. Hence the idea of a "Royal Review." The royal part of you is the one who rightfully wears the crown of wisdom and connection and can see the bigger picture.

The Queen or King of a land takes leadership and sacred responsibility for the welfare and abundance of the land and the people. The best monarchs listen carefully to their subjects and keep an eye out for the health of the land and community. From this higher perspective they can see imbalances as they arise and can correct them before they effect the entire system.

Are you ready to be the Queen or King of your realm? Your kingdom includes the many voices in your head, the different aspects of you and your creations, from your relationships to your work to your health. Your kingdom is vast! And it needs a compassionate, clear ruler. So the Royal Review begins with you reclaiming your crown from whomever may be keeping it hostage (your judge, your victim, your own patterns around needing to be good, your busyness, your boss, your dead father....)

Who has been wearing the crown in your realm? What voice has had the most power in making decisions? It is time for an inner revolution! Take back your crown and consciously choose who wears it. Do you want your ego or your witness wearing those precious jewels? It will take some time to shift the crown bearer to be your most compassionate, creative, wise witness-it-all-with-a-smile self.

The Royal Review is designed to give you the space to head off living by the seat of your pants, getting things done at the last minute, dropping things by mistake energetic. It will help you stop cyclical thinking about what to do next? What to do next? What to do next? By reviewing your lists you will learn to shift towards smooth action maintenance rather than crisis actions.

Robert Pirsig's classic book *Zen and the Art of Motorcycle Maintenance* shows the difference in values between two friends on a cross-country motorcycle journey. One friend is constantly listening into his motorcycle; how does it sound, does it need anything? He focuses on maintenance as a sacred art. His friend drives his motorcycle without care, ignoring potential problems. It is a beautifully written teaching about the importance of mindfulness and presence to the physical realm to avoid drama and emergency.

The Royal Review is sacred maintenance. Avoid using it as a way to feel overwhelmed; you should walk away from any Royal Review with a sense of "I can do this," not with a busier, anxious brain.

Here are some areas/ways to initiate Royal Reviews:

- Review the previous chapters and what you accomplished in putting things into action. What would you like to put more energy towards? How can you keep the Satima teachings alive within you?
- Daily or Weekly: List Review. What did you accomplish, what is still in motion? Have any priorities shifted, or do you have new information

to add?

- Weekly and Quarterly: A financial review to check in on the health and movement of your finances. Any adjustments that need to be made? Monthly or quarterly I recommend working your system for receipts, taxes, etc.
- New or Full Moons: Another sacred cycle marker that you can use for your personal intents or your work lists if you feel inspired by the cycles of the moon.
- Quarterly Reviews: To look over systems, projects, and personal intent. You can link this to the equinoxes and solstices.
- Quarterly or Yearly: A core ideology review for yourself and/or your business is a great practice to do at least once a year.

When you use a cycle to review what you have planted you can gauge the health of your harvest. If you plant a garden and then ignore it you will find it suffers from your neglect. Insects, four-leggeds, lack of water, and weeds will be the logical result. Even knowing this we sometimes expect our work or family gardens to do okay without our nurturing touch and constant care.

Imagine your projects as a part of a vast garden you are the caretender for. Plants thrive on simple attention and presence. When we maintain our connection there is ease in pulling that unwanted weed, or adding extra water to that plant that is getting more sun, or cutting that plant back a bit. We see the signs of distress when we check in regularly with our gardens and can take action to bring relief and balance.

This garden is your life. Enjoy the flowers. Make

choices around what is a weed and what is not. Get your hands dirty.

Deepen into gratitude for the entire process, from seed to harvest. Let's make it ALL sacred!

Resources

Getting Things Done by David Allen. For years this was my rewire-my-life-around-work bible, and I still refer to it regularly. An excellent resource tips, tools, and examples of how to master "The Art of Stress-Free Productivity."

Who Moved My Cheese by Spencer Johnson. An easy read about two mice and two little people and how they deal with change. The humans create a lot of mental activity, the mice are focused on productivity. See what you can learn from a pair of smart mice!

Spiritual Integrity by HeatherAsh Amara and Raven Smith. This book has an excellent chapter on healing the emotional body, along with inspirational support and practical steps to coming into integrity in all areas of your life.

About The Author

HeatherAsh Amara is the co-founder of the Toltec Center of Creative Intent in Austin, TX a non-denominational spiritual community center that offers fabulous classes, workshops, and events. She was trained as a Toltec Mentor by don Miguel Ruiz, author of *The Four Agreements* and is a Sundoor Master Firewalk Instructor.

HeatherAsh is the author of *The Four Elements of Change*, *Toltec Tarot*, and coauthor of *Spiritual Integrity* with her husband, Raven Smith. She is thrilled to share Sacred Time Management after years of experimentation around changing her relationship with time and work.

Photo by R.O. Bumpass

Made in the USA
Charleston, SC
25 October 2011